101 Things®

To Do With A

Jar

101 Things To Do With A Jar

BY BARBARA BEERY

GIBBS SMITH
TO ENRICH AND INSPIRE HUMANKIND

First Edition
23 22 21 20 19   5 4 3 2 1

Published by
Gibbs Smith
P.O. Box 667
Layton, Utah 84041

1.800.835.4993 orders
www.gibbs-smith.com

Designed by Virginia Snow
Printed and bound in Korea

Gibbs Smith books are printed on either recycled, 100% post-consumer
waste, FSC-certified papers or on paper produced from sustainable PEFC-
certified forest/controlled wood source. Learn more at www.pefc.org.

Library of Congress Control Number: 2018968314

ISBN: 978-1-4236-5124-6

A forever thank you to my husband, who has let me turn our home kitchen into a test kitchen for the past 25 years, and who has taste-tested more recipes than I can count.

CONTENTS

Pickles & Jams

Pickled Blueberries or Blackberries 72 • Pickled Strawberries or Raspberries 73 • Pickled Cherries 74 • Pickled Corn 75 • Classic Fridge Pickles 76 • Preserved Lemons 77 • Sweet Berry Jam 78 • Pickled Avocados 79 • Giardiniera 80 • Bloody Mary Pickles 81 • Pickled Peaches, Nectarines, or Apricots 82 • Summer's Best Peachy Plum Jam 83 • Mangolicious Pineapple Hot Pepper Jam 84

Dressings, Condiments & Sauces

Poppy Seed Dressing 86 • Balsamic Vinaigrette 87 • Mediterranean Vinaigrette 88 • Sesame-Soy Dressing 89 • Blue Cheese Dressing 90 • Honey Mustard Dressing 91 • Classic French Vinaigrette 92 • Southern-Style BBQ Spice Blend 93 • Raspberry Vinaigrette 94 • Mexican Spice Blend 95 • Greek Spice Blend 96 • Moroccan Spice Blend 97 • Seeded Honey 98 • Hot Honey 99 • Classic Tomato Sauce 100 • Presto Pesto Sauce 101 • Fettuccini Alfredo Sauce 102 • Asian Peanut Sauce 103 • Herbes de Provence Spice Blend 104

Gift-Giving Jars

M&M's Cookie Mix 106 • Gingerbread Cookie Mix 107 • Homemade Cornbread Mix 108 • Barley Soup Mix 109 • Oatmeal-Chocolate Chip Bread Mix 110 • Happy Birthday Pancake Mix 111 • Curry and Lentil Soup Mix 112 • Old-Fashioned Chicken Noodle Soup Mix 113 • Sweet and Salty Gorp Blend 114 • Cozy as a Blanket Gorp Blend 115 • Monkey Business Gorp Blend 116 • Let's Go to the Movies Gorp Blend 117 • Brownie Mix 118

HELPFUL HINTS

Glass jars are the original reusable, repurposable, and recyclable vessels for holding everything imaginable.

1. **1-2-3 Blender Hack**
Take one standard-mouth jar (a wide-mouth jar won't fit) and a blender with detachable blade base. Place recipe ingredients inside jar. Screw the blender base with blade onto open jar top. Set the ingredient-filled jar on the blender. Blend. VOILA!

2. **Lid Hacks**
Accessories can make your jars more versatile than they already are. Change your jar into a drink container with a reCAP Mason jar lid. Dispense your jar salad dressings with a Mason jar pump lid. Turn your wide-mouth jar into a citrus juicer with a Jarware lid.

3. **Snack Attack**
Start with any size wide-mouth Mason jar and 1 clean fruit cup. Place crackers, granola, cheese cubes, cut veggies, or whatever else you want inside the jar and add the unopened fruit cup, facing up. Secure lid as usual.

4. **Drink Hack**
Place a decorative cupcake liner over drink-filled jar. Secure lid ring over cupcake liner. With a metal skewer, poke a hole in the center of the liner and then insert straw.

5. **Mason Jar Gifts**
Filled jars make great gifts, and there's a whole chapter devoted to them! Decorate the jars with ribbons, baker's twine, or fabrics. Attach small wooden spoons or whisks with ribbon or twine. Include an edible part like an ice cream cone for a dessert sauce.

6. **Glass Jars 101**
- **Mason Glass Jars**—Invented and patented it in 1858 by Mr. Mason, this molded glass jar's mouth has a screw thread on its outer perimeter to accept a metal ring. When screwed down, it presses a separate stamped tin-plated steel disc-shaped lid against the jar's rim. An integral rubber ring on the underside of the lid creates a hermetic seal.
- **Ball Glass Jars**—The Ball brothers took the "ball" and ran with the Mason design in 1884.
- **Kinetic Glass Jars**—Designed with wide mouths, it's easy to add ingredients to these jars while you work. Silicone rings and copper-plated, stainless-steel clamps create an airtight seal to help you preserve your fruits and vegetables. BPA-free glass construction and environmentally friendly.
- **Italian Bormioli Rocco Fido Glass Canning Jars**—With an airtight hinged lid, the Bormioli Rocco Glass Fido Canning Jars are suitable for preserving and storing everything from vegetables to jams.
- **Italian Quattro Stagioni Glass Canning Jars**—The classic design of this jar is enhanced with an embossed motif of a beehive and fresh produce.
- **Le Parfait French Glass Terrines**—Traditional French airtight bail-and-seal closures to hermetically seal out air and moisture. The gaskets are made with hypoallergenic synthetic rubber. Terrines are also great as gift containers for homemade delicacies.
- **Weck**—A German classic since 1900. Unlike other canning jars, Weck jars feature an open tapered shape that's easier to fill and empty, rust-free glass lids (no can opener required), and sealing gaskets that are easy to check at a glance. The jars stack for convenient storage.

DRINKS

CLASSIC LEMONADE

2–3 tablespoons	**sugar** or honey
¼ cup	**hot water**
3 tablespoons	**freshly squeezed lemon juice**
	(about 1–1½ lemons)
¾ cup	**cold water**
	ice
	lemon slices, optional
	fresh mint leaves, optional

In a pint jar, combine the sugar and hot water, and stir until sugar is dissolved. Add the lemon juice and cold water. Fill the jar with ice, secure lid, and shake. Remove lid and garnish with lemon and mint, if desired. Makes 1 serving.

AGUA FRESCAS

1 cup	**water**
1 cup	**chopped fresh fruit,** such as watermelon, cantaloupe, mango, or strawberries
1 teaspoon	**sugar** or agave, to taste
1/2	**lime,** juiced
	ice
	lime, lemon, or orange slices, optional

Combine the water, fruit, and sugar in a quart jar that will fit onto your blender (see page 9). Puree until smooth. Remove from blender, stir in the lime juice, and adjust sugar and lime juice to taste. Add ice. Garnish with lime, if desired. Makes 2 servings.

SPARKLING FRUITY MINT TEA

1 cup **chopped strawberries** or
whole raspberries

¼ cup **mint tea**

½ cup **chilled fruit-flavored sparkling
water** or club soda

fresh mint leaves, optional

chopped fruit or whole
berries, optional

Combine the strawberries with the tea in a pint jar that will fit onto your blender (see page 9). Blend until smooth.

Fill half of a second pint jar with the fruit puree. Top with sparkling water. Stir to blend, garnishing with mint and fruit as desired. Makes 1 serving.

BUTTERFLY PEA TEA

1 cup	**water**
1	**butterfly pea tea bag***
½ teaspoon	**honey**
½ teaspoon	**sugar**
½ teaspoon	**lemon juice**
	ice
	lemon slices, optional

Pour the water into a pint jar and microwave 1–2 minutes, until steaming. Remove jar from microwave and add the tea bag. Steep 1–2 minutes, or until the color is bright blue. Stir in the honey, sugar, and lemon juice. The lemon juice will change the color from blue to purple. Cool for 10 minutes and then add the ice. Serve garnished with lemon, if desired. Makes 1 serving.

* I use Wild Hibiscus Flower Company Tea bags

COLD BREW
VIETNAMESE COFFEE

3 $\frac{1}{2}$	**cups water**
$\frac{1}{2}$ cup	**Cafe du Monde** or any dark roast ground coffee with chicory
2 tablespoons	**condensed milk**
	ice

Add the water and coffee to a quart jar. Secure lid and shake to blend. Place in the refrigerator and steep for 8 hours or overnight. When ready to serve, strain cold brew through a cheesecloth into a clean quart jar to remove grounds. Pour the milk into a pint jar. Add ice and fill to the top with cold brew. Makes 2 servings.

HOMEMADE
HOT CHOCOLATE MIX

6 tablespoons	**powdered creamer**
6 tablespoons	**powdered milk**
6 tablespoons	**powdered sugar**
3 tablespoons	**Dutch cocoa powder**
2 tablespoons	**milk chocolate chips**
½ cup	**mini marshmallows**

In a wide-mouth pint jar, layer the creamer, milk, sugar, and cocoa. Add the chocolate chips and top with the marshmallows. Secure lid.

To make classic hot chocolate, remove the marshmallows from the top of the jar. Stir the powders together in the jar. For 1 serving, combine ½ cup of the mix to 1 cup of boiling water in a pint jar with handle, and stir until completely combined. Top with marshmallows and enjoy. Makes 3 servings.

VARIATIONS:
Peppermint Hot Chocolate: Add 1 tablespoon crushed peppermint per serving.

S'mores Hot Chocolate: Sprinkle 1 crushed graham cracker on top of marshmallows before serving.

GROOVY GREEN SMOOTHIE

2 cups	**fresh spinach**
1 cup	**coconut water** or apple juice
$\frac{1}{2}$ cup	**frozen mango chunks**
$\frac{1}{2}$ cup	**frozen pineapple chunks**
1	**banana,** cut into chunks and frozen
$\frac{1}{2}$	**teaspoon vanilla**

Tightly pack the spinach into a quart jar that will fit onto your blender (see page 9). Add the coconut water, mango, pineapple, banana, and vanilla. Blend until smooth and creamy. Makes 1 serving.

CHERRY LIMEADE

1 cup	**sugar**
½ cup	**freshly squeezed lime juice** (about 4 limes)
½ cup	**tart cherry juice**
1 liter	**club soda** or sparkling water
1 pint	**fresh cherries** (or frozen, if fresh are out of season)
2–3	**limes,** sliced
	ice

Combine the sugar and juices in a gallon jar with spigot. Stir until sugar is completely dissolved. Slowly add the club soda, stirring gently to combine. Add the cherries and limes. Stir once more and serve over ice in 12-ounce jars. Makes 4 servings.

POWER-UP
PURPLE SMOOTHIE

½ cup	**raspberries,** fresh or frozen
½ cup	**blueberries,** fresh or frozen
6	**large strawberries,** fresh or frozen
½ cup	**coconut water**
½ cup	**vanilla Greek yogurt**
I tablespoon	**honey** or maple syrup, to taste
	granola, optional
	fresh berries, optional

Combine all the ingredients in a quart jar that will fit onto your blender (see page 9), and blend until smooth and creamy. Serve with a garnish of granola and berries, if desired. Makes I serving.

LIMONANA (FROZEN MINT LEMONADE)

¼ cup	**freshly squeezed lemon juice** (about 2 lemons)
¼ cup + 2 tablespoons	**ice-cold water**
2–3 tablespoons	**fresh mint**
2–3 tablespoons	**sugar**
2 cups	**ice**
2 sprigs	**mint**

Combine the lemon juice, water, mint, and sugar in a quart jar that will fit onto your blender (see page 9). Blend until the sugar has completely dissolved into the liquid.

Add the ice. Blend on low speed to break up the ice. Then increase the speed and blend until you've reached a uniformly slushy texture. Pour into 2 glasses and place a sprig of mint into each. Serve immediately. Makes 2 servings.

FRESH FRUIT SODAS

3 cups **fresh ripe fruit chunks,** such as strawberries, mangoes, peaches, nectarines, papaya, kiwi, or raspberries

sparkling water or club soda

ice

freshly squeezed lemon juice or lime juice, optional

honey or maple syrup, optional

Place the fruit into a quart jar that will fit onto your blender (see page 9). Puree until completely smooth. Pour the puree into a mesh strainer, using the back of a spoon to push it through into a pint jar. If you don't mind the pulp and tiny seeds, just skip this step and add puree directly to the jar.

In a pint jar, combine 2 tablespoons of puree, 8 ounces of sparkling water, and ice. Adjust to taste with lemon juice or honey, if desired. The fruit puree will keep in a sealed jar in the refrigerator for a week. Makes 16 servings.

CHAI TEA

1 cup	**nonfat dry milk**
1/2 cup	**sugar**
1/2 teaspoon	**ground ginger**
1/2 teaspoon	**ground cardamom**
1/2 teaspoon	**ground cinnamon**
1/4 teaspoon	**ground allspice**
1/8 teaspoon	**ground nutmeg**
1/8 teaspoon	**ground cloves**
dash	**ground red pepper**
	black tea, for serving

Combine all ingredients in a pint jar. Secure lid and shake to blend. Store in an airtight container in the pantry for up to 6 months. For 1 serving, stir 1 1/2 tablespoons tea mix into 8 ounces of hot, freshly brewed black tea. Serves 16.

BASIC SIMPLE SYRUP

1 cup **sugar**
1 cup **water**

Combine the sugar and water in a quart jar and microwave at 30-second intervals, stirring each time to ensure sugar dissolves completely. Remove from microwave and let cool to room temperature. Pour into a pint jar and secure lid. Use to sweeten teas, lemonades, coffees, and hot chocolate, or to dress fresh fruit salads. Refrigerate for up to 2 weeks. Makes 1 ½ cups.

LAVENDER SYRUP

1 cup	**sugar**
1 cup	**water**
3 tablespoons	**dried culinary lavender**

Combine the sugar and water in a quart jar and microwave at 30-second intervals, stirring each time to ensure sugar dissolves completely. Remove from microwave, add the lavender, and steep for 1 hour. Strain into a pint jar and secure lid. Refrigerate for up to 2 weeks. Add to hot or iced teas, coffee, lemonade, or fresh fruit salads. Makes 1 1/2 cups.

VARIATION:
Mint Syrup: Replace the lavender with 1 cup fresh mint leaves.

VANILLA SYRUP

1 cup **sugar**
1 cup **water**
1 **vanilla bean,** split in half lengthwise

Combine sugar and water in a quart jar and microwave at 30-second intervals, stirring each time to ensure sugar dissolves completely. Remove from microwave and add the vanilla bean. Steep for 30 minutes and remove the bean. Pour into a pint jar and secure lid. Refrigerate for up to 2 weeks. Use in coffee, hot tea, and hot chocolate. Makes 1 ½ cups.

VARIATION:
Cinnamon Syrup: Replace the vanilla bean with 4 halved cinnamon sticks.

BREADS, MUFFINS & BREAKFASTS

DOUBLE-CHOCOLATE BANANA BREAD

1 cup	**flour**
1/2 cup	**cocoa powder**
1 teaspoon	**baking soda**
1/2 teaspoon	**sea salt**
3	**ripe bananas** (1 1/2 cups mashed)
1/4 cup	**unsalted butter,** melted and slightly cooled
1/4 cup	**coconut oil,** melted
3/4 cup	**firmly packed light brown sugar**
1	**egg,** room temperature
1 teaspoon	**vanilla**
1 cup	**white chocolate chips,** divided

Preheat oven to 350 degrees. Coat the insides of 6 (8-ounce) jars with softened butter or cooking spray. Dust lightly with flour, shake out excess, and place on a baking sheet. Set aside until ready to use.

In a medium bowl, whisk together the flour, cocoa, baking soda, and salt. Set aside. In a large bowl, mash the bananas with a fork. Add the butter and oil and stir until combined. Stir in the brown sugar, egg, and vanilla. Stir until smooth. Stir dry ingredients into wet ingredients; don't overmix. Fold in 3/4 cup of the chocolate chips.

Pour batter into the prepared jars, filling half full. Sprinkle the remaining 1/4 cup of chocolate chips over the top of the batter, dividing evenly among the jars. Bake for 20–25 minutes, until a toothpick inserted in the middle comes out clean. Transfer to a wire rack to cool completely. Seal with lid and store at room temperature for up to 2 days, in the refrigerator for up to 1 week, or in the freezer for 1 month. Makes 6 servings.

SAVORY BREAKFAST MUFFINS

2 tablespoons	**butter**
¼ cup	**minced fresh chives**
2 cups	**flour**
2 teaspoons	**baking powder**
½ teaspoon	**salt**
2 tablespoons	**sugar**
2	**eggs**
I cup	**milk**
I cup	**grated cheddar cheese**
2–3 slices	**deli ham** or turkey, chopped

Preheat oven to 350 degrees. Coat the insides of 8 (4-ounce) jars with softened butter or cooking spray. Place on a baking sheet and set aside until ready to use.

In a small bowl, microwave the butter until melted. Remove from heat and add the chives. Cool to room temperature and set aside until ready to use.

In a small bowl, combine the flour, baking powder, salt, and sugar. In a large bowl, whisk together the eggs and milk. Add the butter mixture then stir in the cheese and ham. Add dry ingredients to wet ingredients, stirring just until blended. Pour batter into the prepared jars, filling half full.

Bake for 20–25 minutes, until muffin tops are a light brown. Transfer to a wire rack to cool for 5 minutes before serving, or cool completely, seal with lid, and store in the refrigerator for I week or freezer for I month. Makes 8 servings.

HUMMINGBIRD BREAD

2	**eggs**
I cup	**firmly packed light brown sugar**
½ cup	**vegetable oil** or coconut oil
I tablespoon	**vanilla**
3 tablespoons	**buttermilk**
4	**ripe bananas,** mashed
I	**orange,** zested
2 cups	**flour**
½ teaspoon	**ground cinnamon**
¼ teaspoon	**ground cloves**
¼ cup	**shredded sweetened coconut**
¼ cup	**chopped pecans**

Preheat oven to 350 degrees. Coat the insides of 8 (8-ounce) jars with softened butter or cooking spray. Dust lightly with flour, shake out excess, and place on a baking sheet. Set aside until ready to use.

In a large bowl, beat the eggs, brown sugar, oil, vanilla, and buttermilk. Stir in the bananas and orange zest. In a medium bowl, mix together the flour, cinnamon, cloves, coconut, and pecans. Add dry ingredients to wet ingredients and stir to combine.

Pour batter into the prepared jars, filling half full. Bake for 20–25 minutes, until a toothpick inserted in the middle comes out clean. Transfer to a wire rack to cool completely. Seal with lid and store at room temperature for up to 2 days, in the refrigerator for up to I week, or in the freezer for I month. Makes 8 servings.

CRANBERRY-PUMPKIN BREAD

1 1/2 cups	**flour**
2 teaspoons	**baking powder**
1 teaspoon	**salt**
1 teaspoon	**ground cinnamon**
1	**egg**
1/2 cup	**sugar**
1 cup	**pumpkin puree**
6 tablespoons	**butter,** melted
1/4 cup	**maple syrup**
1 teaspoon	**vanilla**
1 teaspoon	**orange zest**
2/3 cup	**dried cranberries**
1/4 cup	**pumpkin seeds**

Preheat oven to 350 degrees. Coat the insides of 8 (8-ounce) jars with softened butter or cooking spray. Dust lightly with flour, shake out excess, and place on a baking sheet. Set aside until ready to use.

In a medium bowl, mix together the flour, baking powder, salt, and cinnamon. In a larger bowl, beat the egg together with the sugar, and then mix in the pumpkin, butter, syrup, vanilla, and orange zest. Add the flour mixture and stir to combine. Fold in the cranberries. Divide the batter equally between jars and garnish evenly with seeds.

Pour batter into the prepared jars, filling half full. Bake for 20–25 minutes, until a toothpick inserted in the middle comes out clean. Transfer to a wire rack to cool completely. Seal with lid and store at room temperature for up to 2 days, in the refrigerator for up to 1 week, or in the freezer for 1 month. Makes 8 servings.

LEMON-POPPY SEED BREAD

2	**lemons,** zested
I cup	**sugar**
½ cup	**buttermilk**
3 tablespoons + 4 teaspoons	**lemon juice,** divided
3	**eggs**
I¾ cup	**flour**
I½ teaspoons	**baking powder**
¼ teaspoon	**baking soda**
¼ teaspoon	**fine sea salt**
⅔ cup	**extra virgin olive oil**
I tablespoon	**poppy seeds**
½ cup	**powdered sugar**

Preheat oven to 350 degrees. Coat the insides of 6 (8-ounce) jars with softened butter or cooking spray. Dust lightly with flour, shake out excess, and place on a baking sheet. Set aside until ready to use.

In a bowl, combine the lemon zest and sugar, and then rub together with your fingers to break down the zest into the sugar. Whisk in the buttermilk, 3 tablespoons lemon juice, and eggs. In another bowl, whisk together the flour, baking powder, baking soda, and salt. Whisk dry ingredients into wet ingredients. Stir in the oil and seeds.

Pour batter into the prepared jars, filling half full. Bake for 20–25 minutes, until a toothpick inserted in the middle comes out clean. Transfer to a wire rack to cool for 10 minutes.

Combine 4 teaspoons lemon juice and the powdered sugar to create a glaze. Brush evenly over the tops of the breads. Allow to cool completely. Seal with lid and store at room temperature for up to 2 days, in the refrigerator for up to I week, or in the freezer for I month. Makes 6 servings.

OVEN-BAKED FRITTATAS

½ cup	**ground breakfast sausage**
2–3	**fingerling** or new potatoes, cubed
1 bunch	**spinach,** stemmed and roughly chopped
	salt and black pepper, to taste
8	**eggs**
¼ cup	**milk**
1 cup	**grated cheese,** such as cheddar or mozzarella

Preheat oven to 375 degrees F. Coat the insides of 6 (½-pint) jars with cooking spray and place on a baking sheet. Set aside until ready to use.

In a large skillet, brown the sausage and break it into crumbles. Add the potatoes and allow to brown lightly on each side about 2–3 minutes, adding a tablespoon of olive oil as necessary to keep from sticking to pan. Remove pan from heat and stir in spinach until slightly wilted, season with salt and pepper.

In a medium bowl, lightly beat the eggs. Season with salt and pepper. Whisk in the milk and cheese. Set aside. Divide the sausage mixture evenly between the jars. Divide eggs evenly between the jars, making sure to leave 1 inch of space at the top of the jar.

Bake for 25–30 minutes, until eggs are set and tops are golden brown. Remove from oven and allow to cool for 5 minutes before serving. If not serving immediately, secure the lid on each jar and refrigerate for up to 2 days. To reheat, warm uncovered in microwave for 1 minute. Makes 6 servings.

BLUEBERRY BREAD

2 ½ cups	**flour**
1 ¼ cups	**sugar**
2 teaspoons	**baking powder**
½ teaspoon	**salt**
2	**eggs**
1 cup	**sour cream**
½ cup	**whole milk**
1 teaspoon	**vanilla**
¾ cup (1 ½ sticks)	**unsalted butter,** melted
1 ½ cups	**blueberries,** fresh or thawed frozen
3 tablespoons	**coarse sugar**

Preheat oven to 350 degrees. Coat the insides of 8 (8-ounce) jars with softened butter or cooking spray. Dust lightly with flour, shake out excess, and place on a baking sheet. Set aside until ready to use.

In a large bowl, whisk the flour, sugar, baking powder, and salt. In a medium bowl, whisk the eggs, sour cream, milk, and vanilla. Add wet ingredients into dry ingredients, and then stir in the butter. Fold in the blueberries. Pour the batter into the prepared jars, filling half full. Sprinkle with the coarse sugar.

Bake for 20–25 minutes, until a toothpick inserted in the middle comes out clean. Transfer to a wire rack to cool completely. Seal with lid and store at room temperature for up to 2 days, in the refrigerator for up to 1 week, or in the freezer for 1 month. Makes 8 servings.

MONKEY BREAD

I tube (16.3 ounces)	**large-size refrigerated biscuits**
¼ cup	**butter,** melted
½ cup	**brown sugar combined with**
	I tablespoon cinnamon

Preheat oven to 400 degrees. Coat the insides of 8 (4-ounce) jars with softened butter or cooking spray. Set aside until ready to use.

Cut each biscuit into 8 pieces. Dip pieces into the butter then roll in cinnamon-sugar mixture. Place 8 biscuit pieces into each jar.

Place jars on a baking sheet and bake for 15–20 minutes, until a toothpick inserted in the middle comes out clean. Remove from oven and cool for 5 minutes. Serve immediately, or cool completely on a wire rack and seal with lid for up to I day. Reheat uncovered in microwave for 15–30 seconds before serving. Makes 8 servings.

WESTERN OMELET

4	**eggs**
⅔ cup	**grated cheddar cheese**
¼ cup	**finely chopped onion**
½ cup	**diced deli ham** or turkey
½ cup	**chopped bell pepper**
	salt and pepper, to taste
1 tablespoon	**snipped chives** or scallions, optional

Coat the insides of 2 (1-pint) jars with cooking spray. Crack 2 eggs into each jar. Divide the cheese, onion, ham, and bell pepper equally between the jars. Season with salt and pepper. Place lids on jars and shake until eggs are well mixed. Remove lids and microwave for 2 minutes, checking every 30 seconds until steamy and puffed above jar top. Garnish with the chives, if desired, and serve. Makes 2 servings.

OVERNIGHT OATS

1/3 cup	**old-fashioned oats**
1/4 teaspoon	**ground cinnamon** or cardamom
	small pinch of salt
1 tablespoon	**chia seeds** or flax seeds
1 tablespoon	**nut butter,** such as peanut, almond, or cashew
1/2–2/3 cup	**milk,** depending on thickness preference
1/2 cup	**fresh fruit,** such as berries, apple, pear, or banana (sliced as needed)
	maple syrup or honey, optional

Combine the oats, cinnamon, salt, seeds, and nut butter in a pint jar. Add a bit of milk to help mix the nut butter into the oats. Add remaining milk to desired thickness and stir well to combine.

If using berries, you can top immediately. If you used more than 1/2 cup milk and you want your fruit to stay on top, wait to top the oats until you're ready to serve. If you're using fruit that will brown when stored, like sliced apple or banana, wait to top the oats until you're ready to serve.

Place the lid on the jar and refrigerate overnight, or up to 5 days. When you're ready to serve, add a drizzle of maple syrup, if desired. Makes 1 serving.

CHIA BREAKFAST PARFAIT

3 tablespoons	**chia seeds**
¾ cup	**milk**
1 teaspoon	**honey** or maple syrup
½ teaspoon	**vanilla**
1 container (8 ounces)	**plain Greek yogurt**
½ cup	**granola**
½ cup	**fresh fruit,** such as berries, apple, pear, or banana (sliced as needed)

To make chia pudding, combine the chia seeds, milk, honey, and vanilla in a pint jar. Secure lid and shake to combine. Refrigerate overnight.

To serve, layer half of the yogurt, chia pudding, granola, and fruit into 2 (1-pint) jars. Repeat the layers and enjoy. Makes 2 servings.

FRENCH TOAST

¼ cup **milk**
1 **egg**
1 teaspoon **ground cinnamon**
1 slice **bread,** cubed
maple syrup, optional

In a pint jar, combine the milk, egg, and cinnamon. Screw on the lid and shake to combine ingredients.

Unscrew lid and add the bread. Press cubes into liquid to ensure all bread cubes are submerged. Screw on lid and shake. Remove lid and microwave the jar at 30-second intervals for 1–2 minutes until steamy and puffed above jar top. Remove from microwave and let cool for a minute or two. Drizzle with maple syrup, if desired, and serve. Makes 1 serving.

MICROWAVE BERRY PANCAKES

1 cup	**flour**
1 tablespoon	**baking powder**
2 tablespoons	**sugar**
2 tablespoons	**margarine,** melted
¾ cup	**milk**
½ cup	**fresh berries,** such as raspberries, blueberries, or strawberries (sliced as needed)
	butter, optional
	fresh berries, optional
	powdered sugar, optional
	maple syrup, optional

Combine the flour, baking powder, and sugar in a small bowl, and whisk until combined. Stir in the margarine and milk until a batter forms. Divide the berries evenly among 2 (1-pint) jars. Spoon in batter, filling no more than half full. Microwave at 30-second intervals for 1–1½ minutes or until steamy and puffed above jar top.

Allow to cool slightly before garnishing with butter, berries, and a dusting of powdered sugar or a drizzle of maple syrup, if desired. Makes 2 servings

GRAB 'N' GO MEALS

BLT SALAD

2 tablespoons	**Honey Mustard Dressing** (page 91)
1 cup	**cooked bow tie pasta**
½ cup	**chopped fresh spinach**
¼ cup	**diced tomatoes**
2 tablespoons	**chopped cooked bacon**

Leaving about 1 inch at the top to allow room for shaking, layer
all ingredients in a wide-mouth quart jar: dressing, pasta, spinach,
tomatoes, and then bacon. Secure lid and store in the refrigerator until
ready to eat, or up to 5 days. To serve, give your jar a few good shakes,
remove lid, and dig in. Makes 1 serving.

ASIAN-INSPIRED SALAD

2 tablespoons	**Sesame-Soy Dressing** (page 89)
½ cup	**cooked,** cooled, and shelled edamame
¼ cup	**thinly sliced red bell pepper**
¼ cup	**thinly sliced yellow bell pepper**
1 cup	**snow peas**
¼ cup	**shredded carrots**
1	**scallion,** chopped
1 cup	**shredded purple cabbage**
1 cup	**chopped romaine lettuce**

Leaving about 1 inch at the top to allow room for shaking, layer all ingredients in a wide-mouth quart jar: dressing, edamame, red bell pepper, yellow bell pepper, snow peas, carrots, scallion, cabbage, and then lettuce. Secure lid on jar and store in the refrigerator until ready to eat, or up to 5 days. To serve, give your jar a few good shakes, remove lid, and dig in. Makes 1 serving.

GREEK SALAD

2–4 tablespoons	**Mediterranean Vinaigrette** (page 88)
1 cup	**cubed cooked chicken**
1/2 cup	**sliced cucumber**
1/3 cup	**crumbled feta cheese**
1/3 cup	**pitted Kalamata olives**
1/2 cup	**chopped tomatoes**

Leaving about 1 inch at the top to allow room for shaking, layer all ingredients in a wide-mouth quart jar: vinaigrette, chicken, cucumber, feta, olives, and then tomatoes. Secure lid on jar and store in the refrigerator until ready to eat, or up to 5 days. To serve, give your jar a few good shakes, remove lid, and dig in. Makes 1 serving.

RAINBOW SALAD

1 cup	**Balsamic Vinaigrette** (page 87)
1 cup	**cooked chickpeas** (if using canned, drained and rinsed)
1/2 cup	**sliced carrots**
1/2 cup	**chopped red bell pepper**
1/2 cup	**chopped yellow bell pepper**
1 cup	**chopped red cabbage**
1/2 cup	**chopped cucumber**
3 cups	**assorted salad greens**
2–3 tablespoons	**raw sunflower seeds**

Leaving about 1 inch at the top to allow room for shaking, layer all ingredients in a wide-mouth quart jar: vinaigrette, chickpeas, carrot, red bell pepper, yellow bell pepper, cabbage, cucumber, greens, and then sunflower seeds. Secure lid on jar and store in the refrigerator until ready to eat, or up to 5 days. To serve, give your jar a few good shakes, remove lid, and dig in. Makes 1 serving.

RASPBERRY BASIL COBB SALAD

	Raspberry Vinaigrette (page 94)
I cup	**cubed cooked chicken**
2 cups	**fresh spinach**
½ cup	**diced cucumber**
½ cup	**diced tomatoes**
2	**hard-boiled eggs,** chopped
4 strips	**bacon,** cooked crispy and finely diced

Leaving about I inch at the top to allow room for shaking, layer all ingredients in a wide-mouth quart jar: vinaigrette, chicken, spinach, cucumber, tomatoes, eggs, and then bacon. Secure lid on jar and store in the refrigerator until ready to eat, or up to 5 days. To serve, give your jar a few good shakes, remove lid, and dig in. Makes I serving.

RED, WHITE, AND BLUEBERRY SALAD

4 tablespoons	**Poppy Seed Dressing** (page 86)
2 cups	**spring mix salad blend**
1 cup	**chopped fresh strawberries**
1/2 cup	**fresh blueberries**
1/2 cup	**crumbled feta cheese**

Leaving about 1 inch at the top to allow room for shaking, layer all ingredients in a wide-mouth quart jar: dressing, salad, strawberries, blueberries, and then cheese. Secure lid on jar and store in the refrigerator until ready to eat, or up to 5 days. To serve, give your jar a few good shakes, remove lid, and dig in. Makes 1 serving.

SOUTHWEST SALAD

½ cup	**salsa**
4 tablespoons	**plain Greek yogurt**
6	**cherry tomatoes,** halved
2	**scallions,** chopped
½ cup	**cooked black beans** (if using canned, drained and rinsed)
½ cup	**frozen corn,** thawed
1	**avocado,** chopped
½ cup	**cubed pepper jack cheese**
2 cups	**chopped romaine lettuce mixed with 2 tablespoons cilantro**

Leaving about 1 inch at the top to allow room for shaking, layer all ingredients in a wide-mouth quart jar: salsa, yogurt, tomatoes, scallions, beans, corn, avocado, cheese, and then lettuce mixture. Secure lid on jar and store in the refrigerator until ready to eat, or up to 5 days. To serve, give your jar a few good shakes, remove lid, and dig in. Makes 1 serving.

PIZZA JARS

1 pound	**pizza dough**
1 cup	**marinara sauce mixed with 2 teaspoons Italian seasoning blend**
2 cups	**grated mozzarella cheese**
	pepperoni slices (optional)

Preheat oven to 375 degrees.

Spray the inside of 8 (half-pint) jars with cooking spray and place on a baking sheet. Place 2 tablespoons of the dough into the bottom of each jar. Press down with fingertips to flatten. Bake for 10 minutes, or until lightly browned. Remove from oven.

Divide the marinara and cheese evenly among the jars, reserving a bit of cheese for a layer of garnish. Add another layer of dough. Garnish with the reserved cheese and pepperoni, if using. Bake for an additional 10 minutes, or until cheese is bubbling. Serve immediately or allow to cool, secure the lid, and refrigerate for up to 2 days. Makes 8 servings.

CORN DOGS

1 packet (7 ounces) **cornbread mix,** plus ingredients listed on package
4 **hot dogs,** halved crosswise

Preheat oven to 375 degrees. Spray the inside of 8 (half-pint) Mason jars and place on a baking sheet. Set aside until ready to use.

Place cornbread batter ingredients into a 1-quart jar. Secure lid and shake well. Divide batter evenly between the prepared jars, filling to $^{1}/_{2}$ inch from the top. Insert 1 hot dog half into the center of each batter-filled jar. Bake for 20 minutes, or until cornbread is light golden brown. Cool on a wire rack for 10 minutes before serving, or let cool completely, secure lid, and refrigerate for up to 5 days. Remove lid and reheat in microwave. Makes 8 servings.

SPICY BLACK BEAN HUMMUS

I can (15 ounces)	**black beans,** drained and rinsed
¼ cup	**fresh salsa**
¼ cup	**fresh cilantro** (including stems)
2 tablespoon	**freshly squeezed lime juice**
I teaspoon	**cumin**
½ teaspoon	**garlic powder**
¼ teaspoon	**chili powder**
¼ teaspoon	**kosher salt**
	vegetables for dipping, such as bell pepper strips, cucumber spears, celery or carrot sticks, and snap peas

Combine the beans, salsa, cilantro, lime juice, cumin, garlic powder, chili powder and salt in a quart jar that will fit onto your blender (see page 9). Process until smooth and creamy. Add I tablespoon of water to thin hummus if necessary. Place 2 tablespoons of hummus into the bottom of 6 (4-ounce) jars and insert veggie dippers. Store sealed in the refrigerator for up to 2 days without veggie dippers. When ready to serve, add veggie dippers. Makes 6 servings.

VIETNAMESE-STYLE CHICKEN NOODLE SOUP

1	**boneless,** skinless chicken breast, boiled and shredded, divided
1 teaspoon	**soy sauce** or tamari, divided
1 teaspoon	**Sriracha,** divided
1/2 teaspoon	**lime juice,** divided
1/2 cup	**chopped broccoli stalks,** divided
1/2 cup	**chopped carrots,** divided
1/2 cup	**chopped red bell pepper,** divided
1/2 cup	**chopped green onions,** divided
2 teaspoons	**chicken** or vegetable bouillon granules, divided
1/2 package (8 ounces)	**rice noodles,** divided
4 sprigs	**cilantro,** divided

Divide the chicken between 2 (1-quart) jars. Add half the soy sauce, Sriracha, and lime juice to each jar. Layer the broccoli, carrots, bell pepper, and green onions in each jar. Top with the bouillon followed by the noodles and cilantro. Seal and refrigerate until ready to serve, up to 5 days. To serve, pour in boiling water to fill about two-thirds of the jar and stir contents well. Microwave, uncovered, for 1–2 minutes, until heated through. Serve immediately. Makes 2 servings.

VARIATION: For a classic American Chicken Noodle Soup, substitute equal amounts Worcestershire sauce for the soy and Sriracha, lemon juice for lime juice, egg noodles for rice noodles, and parsley for cilantro.

ITALIAN WHITE BEAN HUMMUS

I can (15 ounces)	**cannellini beans,** drained and rinsed
2 cloves	**garlic**
2 tablespoons	**freshly squeezed lemon juice**
1/3 cup	**olive oil,** plus up to 3 tablespoons more depending on desired texture
1/4 cup	**fresh Italian parsley**
	salt and pepper, to taste
	vegetables for dipping, such as bell pepper strips, cucumber spears, celery or carrot sticks, and snap peas

Combine the beans, garlic, lemon juice, olive oil, and parsley in a 32-ounce jar that will fit onto your blender (see page 9). Process until the mixture is coarsely chopped. Season with salt and pepper. Place 2 tablespoons of hummus into the bottom of 6 (4-ounce) jars and insert veggie dippers. Store sealed in the refrigerator for up to 2 days without veggie dippers. When ready to serve, add veggie dippers. Makes 6 servings.

GUACAMOLE HUMMUS

2	**avocados**
I can (15 ounces)	**chickpeas,** rinsed and drained
I clove	**garlic,** minced
I tablespoon	**freshly squeezed lemon juice** or lime juice
I tablespoon	**olive oil**
	salt and pepper, to taste
	vegetables for dipping, such as bell pepper strips, cucumber spears, celery or carrot sticks, and snap peas

Dice I avocado and set aside until ready to use. Slice the remaining avocado.

Combine the sliced avocado, chickpeas, garlic, citrus juice, olive oil, salt, and pepper in a 32-ounce jar that will fit onto your blender (see page 9). Process until smooth and creamy. Remove jar from blender and gently fold in diced avocado. Place 2 tablespoons of hummus into the bottom of 6 4-ounce jars and insert veggie dippers. Store sealed in the refrigerator for up to 2 days without veggie dippers. When ready to serve, add veggie dippers. Store sealed in the refrigerator for up to 2 days. Makes 6 servings.

DESSERTS

FRUIT COBBLERS

2 1/2 cups	**fresh fruit,** such as diced apples or pears, blueberries, blackberries, or sliced peaches
I teaspoon	**vanilla**
1/2 cup	**flour**
1/2 cup	**sugar**
1/2 teaspoon	**salt**
1/2 teaspoon	**ground cinnamon,** nutmeg, cardamom, or ginger
4 tablespoons	**butter,** cut into 8 pieces

Preheat oven to 350 degrees. Spray the inside of 8 wide-mouth jars with cooking spray and place on a baking sheet. Set aside until ready to use.

Toss the fruit and vanilla together in a bowl. Equally portion fruit into each jar. In a measuring cup, combine the flour, sugar, salt, and cinnamon. Pour equally over the top of each fruit-filled jar. Place I tablespoon of butter on top of batter in each jar. Bake for 20–25 minutes, until the top is golden brown and the fruit is bubbling. Cool completely, secure lid, and serve within a few hours, or refrigerate for up to 3 days. To reheat, remove lid and heat in microwave at 30 second intervals until steamy and heated through. Makes 8 servings.

FRUIT CRISPS

2 cups	**granola** (the kind with clumps)
1/4 teaspoon	**salt**
2 tablespoons	**melted butter**
2 1/2 cups	**fresh fruit,** such as diced apples or pears, blueberries, blackberries, or sliced peaches
1 cup	**sugar**
1/2 teaspoon	**ground cinnamon** or nutmeg

Preheat oven to 350 degrees. Spray the inside of 8 wide-mouth jars with cooking spray and place on a baking sheet. Set aside until ready to use. Combine the granola and salt with the butter in a bowl. Set aside until ready to use

Toss the fruit, sugar, and cinnamon together in a bowl. Spoon equal amounts of the fruit into each jar and top with granola mixture. Bake for 25–30 minutes, until crust is lightly browned and fruit is bubbling. Makes 8 servings.

JAR LID TINY TARTS

I package (14 ounces)	**refrigerated pie crusts**
½ cup	**raspberry jam**
I small box	**chocolate** or vanilla pudding mix (not instant), cooked and chilled, or I jar (10 ounces) lemon curd
24	**fresh raspberries**
	powdered sugar, for dusting

Place 8 wide-mouth Mason jar lids with the rubber strip facing down in their rims on a parchment-lined baking sheet. Spray with cooking spray.

Cut out 8 pie crust rounds about ¼ inch larger than the jar lid bottom. Prick crusts with a fork and refrigerate for 30 minutes. While pie crusts are chilling, preheat oven to 375 degrees.

Remove crusts from refrigerator and bake for 10−12 minutes, until the edges of the crust are golden brown. Cool completely on a wire rack, but do not remove crusts from the lids.

Place approximately I teaspoon of jam onto the bottom of each tart and spread across the bottom. Fill each tart with pudding and garnish with 2−3 raspberries. Refrigerate for at least I hour, or up to I day. Remove tarts from lids, dust with powdered sugar, and serve. Makes 8 servings.

JAR LID FRUIT PIES

4	**refrigerated pie crusts**
1 can (21 ounces)	**fruit pie filling,** of choice
4 tablespoons	**melted butter**
1 tablespoon	**sugar**

Preheat the oven to 375 degrees. Line a baking sheet with parchment paper and place 10 jar lids on top. Spray lids with cooking spray and set aside until ready to use.

Cut out twenty 3 1/4-inch circles out of the pie crusts. Place 1 crust inside each lid, making sure to press around the bottom so that the crust hugs the inside of the lids. Spoon approximately 3 tablespoons of filling into each crust and cover with an additional crust. Dip your fingers in water and crease the crusts together. Drizzle the butter on top of each mini pie, and then sprinkle with the sugar. Bake for 25–30 minutes, until golden brown on top. Cool on a wire rack for 10–15 minutes before removing pies from lids. Makes 10 servings.

NO-BAKE FRUITY CHEESECAKES

1 ½ cups	**graham cracker crumbs**
6 tablespoons	**melted butter**
⅓ cup	**sugar**
1 package (8 ounces)	**cream cheese,** softened
1 can (14 ounces)	**sweetened condensed milk**
⅓ cup	**freshly squeezed lemon juice**
1 teaspoon	**vanilla**
1 can (21 ounces)	**blueberry, strawberry, or cherry pie filling**
½ teaspoon	**almond extract**

Mix the graham crackers, butter, and sugar together. Press mixture into the bottom of 12 (half-pint) jars. Place on a baking sheet and chill in refrigerator for 1 hour.

Beat the cream cheese until fluffy. Gradually add the condensed milk until combined. Stir in the lemon juice and vanilla. Pour over the chilled crust and chill in the refrigerator for 3 hours. Add fruit topping just before serving. Open the fruit filling can, add the almond extract, and stir well. Spoon the filling over top of each cheesecake. Cheesecakes without fruit topping may be covered and stored for up to 2 days. Makes 12 servings.

COOKIES AND CREAM CUPCAKES

1 box (15 ounces)	**chocolate cake mix,** plus ingredients listed on package
1 container (15 ounces)	**vanilla frosting**
1 package (3 ounces)	**mini Oreo cookies**

Preheat oven to 350 degrees. Spray the inside of 24 (4-ounce) jars with cooking spray and place on a baking sheet. Set aside until ready to use.

Prepare the cake mix according to package directions. Divide batter evenly between jars, leaving 1 inch of space at the top. Wipe out any batter that clings to the side to prevent burning. Bake cupcakes according to package directions, 18–22 minutes, and cool completely on a wire rack before sealing.

Before serving, remove lids, frost with vanilla frosting, and place 1 cookie on top of each cupcake. Sealed, unfrosted cupcakes will keep for up to 5 days in the refrigerator. Makes 24 servings.

NO-BAKE KEY LIME PIES

1 ½ cups	**graham cracker crumbs**
⅓ cup	**sugar**
6 tablespoons	**melted butter**
1 package (8 ounces)	**cream cheese,** softened
1 can (14 ounces)	**sweetened condensed milk**
¾ cup	**freshly squeezed key lime juice**
¾–1 ½ cups	**Whipped Cream** (page 69)
2–3	**key limes,** thinly sliced (optional)

Mix the graham crackers, sugar, and butter together. Press mixture into the bottom of 12 (4-ounce) jars. Place on a baking sheet and chill in refrigerator for 1 hour.

Beat together the cream cheese, condensed milk, and lime juice until smooth and creamy. Chill in the refrigerator for 30 minutes.

Remove crusts and filling from refrigerator and spoon equally into each jar. Top filling in each jar with 1–2 tablespoons whipped cream and garnish with a lime slice, if using. Serve immediately, or secure lid and store in refrigerator up to 1 day. Makes 12 servings.

COOKIE AND
ICE CREAM JARS

1 ½ cups   **crushed chocolate** or vanilla wafer
cookies or graham crackers

6 tablespoons   **butter,** melted

1 pint   **vanilla ice cream**

1 pint   **chocolate ice cream**

Chocolate Sauce (page 68)

Whipped Cream (optional, page 69)

sprinkles (optional)

Place 8 wide-mouth (half-pint) jars on a baking sheet. Combine the cookie crumbs and butter in a bowl. Spoon equally into the bottom of each jar and freeze for 30 minutes.

Bring the ice cream out of the freezer about 15 minutes before scooping into jars. Place 1 scoop of vanilla ice cream onto frozen crust, followed by a layer of sauce, and 1 scoop of chocolate ice cream. Secure lid and freeze for at least 2 hours, or until ready to serve, up to 24 hours. Garnish with whipped cream and sprinkles, if using, before serving. Makes 8 servings.

LEMON MERINGUE PIES

½ cup	**graham cracker crumbs**
3 tablespoons + 2 teaspoons	**sugar,** divided
2 tablespoons	**melted butter**
1 can (14 ounces)	**sweetened condensed milk**
3	**eggs,** separated
½ cup	**freshly squeezed lemon juice**
1	**lemon,** zested
¼ teaspoon	**cream of tartar**

Place 6 (half-pint) jars on a baking sheet and set aside until ready to use.

In a medium bowl, combine the graham crackers, 2 teaspoons of the sugar, and the butter. Divide crumb mixture evenly between the jars. In another bowl, whisk together the condensed milk, egg yolks, lemon juice, and zest. Divide lemon mixture evenly between jars and place in refrigerator while making meringue.

Preheat oven to 350 degrees.

Place the egg whites and cream of tartar in a bowl and beat with a hand mixer until frothy. With the mixer still running, very, very slowly add the remaining sugar, 1 teaspoon at a time, beating until stiff peaks form. Spoon the meringue evenly over the lemon filling in each jar. Bake for 10–12 minutes, until the meringue is golden. Cool completely on a wire rack and then refrigerate for at least 2 hours before serving. Makes 6 servings.

TIE-DYE RAINBOW CUPCAKES

1 box (15 ounces)	**white cake mix,** plus ingredients listed on package
	green, blue, red, and orange gel paste food colorings
1 container (15 ounces)	**vanilla frosting**
1/2 cup	**rainbow sprinkles**

Preheat oven to 350 degrees. Spray the inside of 24 (4-ounce) jars with cooking spray and place on a baking sheet. Set aside until ready to use.

Prepare the cake mix according to package directions. Divide batter evenly between 4 small bowls, adding 1 color to each of the 4 bowls (follow the instructions on the coloring package for appropriate amounts). Mix well. Divide each batter evenly between the jars, leaving 1 inch of space at the top. Wipe out any batter that clings to the side to prevent burning. Bake cupcakes according to package directions, 18–22 minutes, and cool completely on a wire rack before sealing. Sealed, unfrosted cupcakes will keep for up to 5 days in the refrigerator.

Before serving, remove lids, frost with vanilla frosting, and sprinkle evenly with rainbow sprinkles. Makes 24 servings.

VARIATIONS:
Gingerbread Cupcakes: Leave out the food coloring, substitute cinnamon frosting for vanilla, and decorate with red and green sprinkles and mini gingerbread men.

Pink Velvet Cupcakes: Add just enough red food coloring to make pink batter and pale pink icing. Decorate with heart sprinkles.

CLASSIC TRIFLE JARS

1	**prepared angel food cake** or pound cake, cubed
1 box (3.4 ounces)	**instant vanilla pudding,** plus milk for preparing
1 cup	**raspberry** or strawberry jam
1 cup	**fresh raspberries** or strawberries
1 cup	**fresh blueberries** or blackberries
1 cup	**Whipped Cream** (page 69)

Layer cake cubes, vanilla pudding, jam, berries alternating layers, and top with whipped cream equally into 6 ($^1/_2$-pint) jars. Secure lid and refrigerate 2 hours prior to serving. If storing in fridge overnight, garnish with whipped cream right before serving. For a chocolate trifle, substitute 1 chocolate cake, 1 box instant chocolate pudding, and substitute chocolate or caramel sauce for the jam. Makes 6 servings.

HOMEMADE MAGIC SHELL

I cup	**milk chocolate chips**
3 tablespoons	**coconut oil**

Place chocolate chips and coconut oil into a wide-mouth pint jar. Microwave in 30 second intervals, stirring between each time until completely melted. Seal and store at room temperature or in the refrigerator for up to 3 months. If solidified, heat briefly in microwave before using. Use on ice cream and ice cream cones or to make chocolate-covered bananas or strawberries. Makes a generous I cup.

VARIATIONS:
Fruity Magic Shell: Replace milk chocolate chips with white chocolate chips plus 2 tablespoons finely crushed freeze-dried strawberries or raspberries.

Matcha Magic Shell: Replace milk chocolate chips with white chocolate chips plus 2 teaspoons matcha powder.

CHOCOLATE SAUCE

I cup	**cocoa powder**
I ½ cups	**sugar**
I cup	**water**
I tablespoon	**butter**
	pinch of salt
I teaspoon	**vanilla**

Place the cocoa powder, sugar, and water into a wide-mouth quart jar. Secure lid and shake well. Remove lid and microwave at 30-second intervals, shaking to combine, until mixture boils. Remove from microwave, add the butter, salt, and vanilla. Stir to combine. Allow to cool, secure lid, and store in the refrigerator for up to I month. Reheat briefly in microwave before serving. Makes a generous I cup.

WHIPPED CREAM

1 cup	**heavy cream**
1–2 tablespoons	**powdered sugar,** to taste
1 teaspoon	**vanilla**

Place a pint jar with lid secured in the freezer for 30 minutes. Remove jar from freezer, remove lid, and add the cream, sugar, and vanilla. Secure lid and shake vigorously for at least 5 minutes. Remove lid to check consistency. If cream is not thick enough, shake a little longer, but not too long or it will turn to butter! Store in refrigerator for up to 1 day.

CREME BRULEE JARS

10	**egg yolks,** room temperature
¹/₂ cup	**sugar**
2¹/₂ cups	**whipping cream,** room temperature
1 tablespoon	**vanilla**
¹/₄ cup	**sugar,** for caramelizing tops after cooking

Preheat oven to 300 degrees.

In a large mixing bowl, beat together the egg yolks with the sugar until the sugar is dissolved and the mixture is a pale yellow. Add the whipping cream and vanilla and whisk until well-blended.

Fill 12 (4-ounce) jars within ¹/₄ inch from the top and place the filled jars into a 9 x 13-inch roasting pan with sides. Carefully pour in hot water so that it almost reaches the top of jars. Bake until set, about 55 minutes. Carefully remove pan from oven and leave in the water bath until cooled.

Remove jars from water bath, wipe water off, and place in refrigerator to chill for at least 2 hours.

Prior to serving, remove from refrigerator and sprinkle about 2 teaspoons of sugar over each custard top. Using a small hand-held torch, melt the sugar until a burnt caramel is made. If you don't have a torch, place under the broiler until sugar melts. Refrigerate again, for up to 6 hours, or serve immediately. Makes 12 servings.

PICKLES
& JAMS

PICKLED BLUEBERRIES OR BLACKBERRIES

I cup	**red wine vinegar**
¼ cup	**sugar** (plus 2 tablespoons sugar if using blackberries)
I ½ teaspoons	**kosher salt**
I pint	**fresh blueberries** or blackberries
I	**shallot** or small red onion, sliced

In a bowl, mix together the vinegar, sugar, and salt until dissolved. Place the blueberries and shallot into a wide-mouth quart jar. Pour liquid over fruit, leaving I inch of space at the top of the jar, and secure lid. Discard any remaining pickling liquid. Place in refrigerator for a minimum of 24 hours and up to 5 days. (Flavors intensify as the fruit "pickles," so process for at least 3 days if time allows.) Both berries make a great addition to a charcuterie board and add a sweet tartness to green salads. Makes I quart.

PICKLED STRAWBERRIES OR RASPBERRIES

1 cup	**balsamic vinegar**
½ cup	**water**
¼ cup	**maple syrup**
1 tablespoon	**kosher salt**
1	**vanilla bean,** split in half lengthwise, or 2 teaspoons vanilla
1 pound	**strawberries,** hulled and sliced

In a medium saucepan, bring the vinegar, water, syrup, and salt to a simmer, stirring to dissolve the salt. Remove from heat and add the vanilla bean. Cool for 15 minutes and pour into a measuring cup with spout. Place the strawberries in a wide-mouth quart jar. Pour liquid over strawberries, leaving 1 inch of space at the top of the jar, and secure lid. Discard any remaining pickling liquid. Allow to cool completely and refrigerate for a minimum of 24 hours and up to 5 days. (Flavors intensify as the fruit "pickles," so process for at least 3 days if time allows.) These berries add a sweet tartness to green salads and are delicious on fruit sorbets or pound cake. Makes 1 quart.

PICKLED CHERRIES

¾ cup	**apple cider vinegar**
¾ cup	**water**
¼ cup	**dark brown sugar**
2 teaspoons	**whole black peppercorns**
1	**cinnamon stick,** broken in half
1 pound	**fresh cherries,** stemmed, and pitted
5 sprigs	**fresh thyme**

In a medium saucepan, combine the vinegar, water, brown sugar, peppercorns, and cinnamon stick. Bring to a simmer, stirring until the sugar dissolves. Reduce heat to low and add the cherries and thyme. Cook for 5 minutes, or until the cherries have just started to soften. Remove from heat and allow to cool for 15 minutes.

Spoon the cherries into a wide-mouth quart jar. Pour remaining liquid into a measuring cup with spout and pour over the cherries, leaving 1 inch of space at the top of the jar. Secure lid. Discard any remaining pickling liquid. Allow to cool completely and refrigerate for a minimum of 24 hours and up to 2 weeks. (Flavors intensify as the fruit "pickles," so process for at least 3 days if time allows.) Excellent in lemonade or on top of ice cream or yogurt. Makes 1 quart.

NOTE: You can either remove the peppercorns, cinnamon stick, and thyme before placing the cherries into the jar, or leave them with the cherries for a stronger flavor.

PICKLED CORN

¾ cup	**white vinegar**
½ cup	**water**
⅓ cup	**sugar**
1 tablespoon	**kosher salt**
1 ½ cups	**fresh corn** (2–3 ears)
½–1	**jalapeno** or serrano pepper, halved lengthwise
1	**fresh bay leaf,** torn in half

In a small pot, stir together the vinegar, water, sugar, and salt. Bring to a boil, stirring occasionally. Remove from heat and cool for 15 minutes. Pour the liquid into a measuring cup with a spout. Place the corn, jalapeno, and bay leaf into a pint jar. Pour liquid over corn, leaving 1 inch of space at the top of the jar. Secure lid. Discard any remaining pickling liquid. Allow to cool completely then refrigerate for a minimum of 24 hours and up to 2 weeks. (Flavors intensify as the corn "pickles," so process for at least 3 days if time allows.) Pickled corn is great on any Mexican food and is especially good stirred into your favorite guacamole or mixed into pasta or potato salad. Makes 1 pint.

CLASSIC FRIDGE PICKLES

1 ½ cups	**water**
⅔ cup	**apple cider vinegar**
1 tablespoon	**sugar**
2 teaspoons	**kosher salt**
1 teaspoon	**mustard seeds**
2 cloves	**garlic,** thinly sliced
2 sprigs	**dill**
6–8	**Persian cucumbers** or pickling cucumbers, quartered lengthwise

Place the water, vinegar, sugar, salt, mustard seeds, garlic, and dill in a quart jar. Shake until sugar and salt are dissolved. Add the cucumbers, secure lid, and refrigerate for a minimum of 24 hours and up to 2 weeks. (Flavors intensify as the cucumbers "pickle," so process for at least 3 days if time allows.) Makes 1 quart.

PRESERVED LEMONS

I cup	**kosher salt**
½ cup	**sugar**
5	**Meyer lemons**

Combine the salt and sugar in a medium bowl. Cut lemons lengthwise into quarters. Pack alternating layers of salt mixture and lemons into a quart glass jar. Cover and chill, shaking every day for the first 2 weeks of curing to redistribute brine. Allow lemons to brine for at least I month. They will keep for up to I year. Use preserved lemons in salad dressings, sauces, salsas, dips, and, of course, the classic chicken tagine. Makes I quart.

SWEET BERRY JAM

I pound	**fresh raspberries**
I pound	**fresh strawberries,** hulled
I pound	**fresh blackberries**
3 ½ cups	**sugar**
¼ teaspoon	**kosher salt**
2 tablespoons	**freshly squeezed lemon juice**

Stir together the berries, sugar, and salt in a large heavy-bottom pot. Bring to a boil, stirring until sugar is dissolved. Mash the fruit with a potato masher as it cooks. Add the lemon juice and continue to boil, stirring frequently, for about 10–15 minutes. Mixture is ready when it clings to a spoon. Remove from heat, and if there is any foam on top, skim off with a spoon and discard. Cool for 15 minutes and ladle equally into 3 (1-pint) jars, leaving ¾ inch of space at the top of the jar. Cool completely and secure lid. Refrigerate for up to 1 month, or freeze for up to 1 year. Makes 3 pints.

VARIATION: Add 1 3-inch sprig of mint or 5 basil leaves to fruit mixture before boiling. Remove cooked herbs before ladling jam into jars.

PICKLED AVOCADOS

1 cup	**apple cider vinegar**
1 cup	**water**
1/3 cup	**sugar**
1 tablespoon	**kosher salt**
1 tablespoon	**black peppercorns**
1 tablespoon	**mustard seeds**
1 teaspoon	**crushed red pepper**
1 clove	**garlic,** thinly sliced
10 sprigs	**cilantro** or Italian parsley
2	**very firm avocados,** peeled and sliced

In a saucepan over medium heat, combine the vinegar, water, sugar, and salt. Bring to a boil, stirring occasionally. When the sugar and salt have dissolved, remove from heat and cool for 15 minutes. Pour liquid into a measuring cup with a spout.

Place the peppercorns, mustard seeds, red pepper, garlic, cilantro, and avocados into a pint jar. Pour cooled pickling mixture into the jar, leaving 1 inch of space at the top of the jar, and secure with lid. Discard any remaining pickling liquid. Allow to cool completely then refrigerate for a minimum of 3 hours and up to 1 week. (Flavors intensify as the avocados "pickle," so process for at least 24 hours if time allows.) Use in tacos, on sandwiches, or on avocado toast. Excellent for making guacamole too. Makes 1 pint.

GIARDINIERA

½ cup	**red wine vinegar**
1 tablespoon	**kosher salt**
1 teaspoon	**dried oregano**
1	**bay leaf**
1 clove	**garlic,** mashed
⅓ cup	**olive oil**
2 cups	**water**
1 cup	**broccoli florets**
1 cup	**chopped carrots**
1 cup	**chopped celery**
1 cup	**chopped orange bell pepper**
¼ cup	**pitted and coarsely chopped green olives**

In a large saucepan, combine the vinegar, salt, oregano, bay leaf, garlic, olive oil and water. Bring to a simmer, stirring occasionally. Add the broccoli and cook for 1 minute. Remove from heat. Add the carrots, celery, bell pepper, and olives. Let cool for 15 minutes. Spoon veggies into a wide-mouth quart jar. Pour the liquid into a measuring cup with a spout. Transfer liquid into veggie-filled jar, leaving 1 inch of space at the top of the jar. Discard any remaining pickling liquid you may have left. Secure lid and place in refrigerator for at least 24 hours and up to 2 weeks. (Flavors intensify as the veggies "pickle," so process for at least 3 days if time allows.) Makes 1 quart.

BLOODY MARY PICKLES

1/3 cup	**Zing Zang Bloody Mary Mix**
2 tablespoons	**freshly squeezed lemon juice**
2 teaspoons	**prepared horseradish**
1/2 teaspoon	**black peppercorns**
1/2 teaspoon	**kosher salt**
Dash or 2	**of Tabasco hot sauce**
1/4 cup	**white wine vinegar**
3	**small Persian cucumbers** or pickling cucumbers, ends trimmed and quartered lengthwise
3	**round slices fresh lemon**
1 clove	**garlic,** sliced in half

In a small saucepan over medium heat, combine the Bloody Mary mix, lemon juice, horseradish, peppercorns, kosher salt, and hot sauce. Bring to a boil, stirring occasionally, and then remove from heat. Stir in the vinegar. Cool for 15 minutes and pour into a measuring cup with spout.

Pack the cucumbers, lemon, and garlic into a pint jar. Pour liquid over cucumber mix, leaving 1 inch of space at the top of the jar. Secure lid. Discard any remaining pickling liquid. Allow to cool completely and refrigerate for a minimum of 24 hours and up to 2 weeks. (Flavors intensify as the cucumbers "pickle," so process for at least 3 days if time allows.) These are spicy little rascals, so cut back on the Tabasco or horseradish to taste. Excellent on a charcuterie board along with mild cheeses like Havarti and Muenster. Makes 1 pint.

PICKLED PEACHES, NECTARINES, OR APRICOTS

1 1/4 cups	**rice vinegar**
1/4 cup + 3 teaspoons	**maple syrup**
1/4 cup	**sugar**
1/2 teaspoon	**ground cinnamon**
1/4 teaspoon	**ground nutmeg**
1 (1 inch) piece	**fresh ginger,** peeled and cut into thick slices
3–4	**ripe, firm fresh peaches** or nectarines, or 5–6 fresh apricots, sliced

In a medium saucepan, bring the vinegar, syrup, sugar, cinnamon, and nutmeg to a simmer, stirring to dissolve sugar. Remove from heat and allow to cool for 15 minutes.

Pour into a measuring cup with spout. Place the ginger on the bottom of a wide-mouth quart jar and top with fruit. Pour liquid over the fruit, leaving 1 inch of space at the top of the jar, and secure lid. Discard any remaining pickling liquid. Allow to cool completely and refrigerate for a minimum of 24 hours and up to 2 weeks. (Flavors intensify as the fruit "pickles," so process for at least 3 days if time allows.) These are outstanding on ice cream or yogurt or alongside baked ham or turkey. Makes 1 quart.

SUMMER'S BEST PEACHY PLUM JAM

1 1/2 pounds	**peaches,** peeled and pitted
1 1/2 pounds	**plums,** peeled and pitted
3 1/2 cups	**sugar**
1/4 teaspoon	**kosher salt**
2 tablespoons	**freshly squeezed orange juice**

Stir together the peaches, plums, sugar, and salt in a large heavy-bottom pot. Bring to a boil, stirring until sugar is dissolved. Mash the fruit as it cooks with a potato masher. Add the orange juice and continue to boil, stirring frequently, for about 10–15 minutes. Mixture is ready when it clings to a spoon. Remove from heat, and if there is any foam on top, skim off with a spoon and discard. Cool for 15 minutes and ladle equally into 3 (1-pint) jars, leaving 3/4 inch of space at the top of the jar. Cool completely and secure lid. Refrigerate for up to 1 month.

VARIATIONS:
Peach Vanilla Jam, Stir in 1 teaspoon of vanilla extract after the fruit mixture has been cooked. It's great as an ice cream topping.

Peach Herb Jam: Use 3 pounds of peaches and cook mixture with 4 large sprigs of rosemary. Remove herbs before ladling into jars. This makes a great glaze for grilled pork tenderloin and chicken.

MANGOLICIOUS PINEAPPLE HOT PEPPER JAM

I cup	**finely chopped mango**
I cup	**finely chopped pineapple**
⅔ cup	**chopped jalapeno,** serrano, or shishito (this variety is milder) peppers
⅔ cup	**water**
I	**lemon,** juiced
3 tablespoons	**low-sugar pectin**
I cup	**sugar**

Combine the mango, pineapple, peppers, water, lemon juice, and pectin in a heavy-bottom saucepan. Bring to a boil, stirring occasionally. Lower heat and stir in sugar. Bring mixture back to a boil, stirring constantly for 1–2 minutes. Remove from heat and cool for 15 minutes. Ladle into 2 (1-pint) jars, leaving ¾ inch of space at the top of each jar. Secure lid. Cool completely. Refrigerate for up to 1 month. This makes a great appetizer served over softened goat cheese with tortilla chips. Makes 2 (1-pint) jars.

DRESSINGS, CONDIMENTS & SAUCES

POPPY SEED DRESSING

¼ cup	**white wine vinegar** or champagne vinegar
¼	**cup sugar**
1	**small shallot,** finely minced
1–1½ tablespoons	**poppy seeds**
½ teaspoon	**salt**
½ teaspoon	**ground mustard**
½ cup	**olive oil,** grapeseed oil, or a mix
2 teaspoons	**mayonnaise** (optional for a creamier dressing)

Combine the vinegar and sugar in a pint jar. Secure lid and shake until sugar is mostly dissolved. Add the shallot, poppy seeds, salt, mustard, oil, and mayonnaise if using. Secure lid and shake to combine. Store sealed jar in refrigerator for up to 2 weeks. Remove from the refrigerator 5 minutes before using and shake well before serving. Excellent on fruit salads, spinach salads, and chicken or pasta salads. Makes 1 cup.

BALSAMIC VINAIGRETTE

¼ cup	**balsamic vinegar**
2 tablespoons	**honey**
I tablespoon	**Dijon mustard**
½ teaspoon	**salt**
I	**large clove garlic,** minced
	salt and pepper, to taste
¾ cup	**extra virgin olive oil**

Combine all ingredients except olive oil in a pint jar, secure lid, and shake. Remove lid, add olive oil, secure lid, and shake vigorously to emulsify. Store sealed jar in refrigerator for up to 2 weeks. Excellent on all salads and delicious drizzled on roasted vegetable or as a marinade. Versatile. Makes I cup.

MEDITERRANEAN VINAIGRETTE

4 tablespoons	**red wine vinegar**
2 tablespoons	**freshly squeezed lemon juice**
1 tablespoon	**lemon zest**
1 teaspoon	**Cavender's All Purpose Greek Seasoning**
1 teaspoon	**dried oregano**
	salt and pepper, to taste
½ cup	**olive oil**

Combine all ingredients except olive oil in a pint jar, secure lid, and shake. Remove lid, add olive oil, secure lid, and shake vigorously to emulsify. Store sealed jar in refrigerator for up to 1 week. Excellent on salads that include Kalamata olives, cucumbers, and tomatoes, on all grains and grain salads, and as a marinade for chicken. Makes scant 1 cup.

SESAME-SOY DRESSING

2 tablespoons	**soy sauce**
2 tablespoons	**freshly squeezed lemon juice**
2 teaspoons	**honey**
1 teaspoon	**grated fresh ginger**
1 clove	**garlic,** finely minced
1 teaspoon	**sesame seeds**
2 1/2 tablespoons	**grapeseed oil** or canola oil
	salt and pepper, to taste
1/2 tablespoon	**sesame oil**

Combine all ingredients except sesame oil in a pint jar, secure lid, and shake. Remove lid, add olive oil, secure lid, and shake vigorously to emulsify. Store sealed jar in refrigerator for up to 1 week. Great tossed in salads with greens, citrus, and almonds as well as on soba noodles and rice. Makes scant 1 cup.

BLUE CHEESE DRESSING

1 teaspoon	**freshly squeezed lemon juice**
1 teaspoon	**white wine vinegar**
1 tablespoon	**finely minced onion**
1 teaspoon	**finely minced garlic**
2 tablespoons	**finely chopped fresh parsley**
	salt and pepper, to taste
1/3 cup	**mayonnaise**
1/3 cup	**sour cream**
1/3 cup	**crumbled blue cheese**

Combine the lemon juice, vinegar, onion, garlic, and parsley in a pint jar. Season with salt and pepper. Secure lid and shake. Remove lid, add mayonnaise and sour cream, secure lid, and shake vigorously to emulsify. Stir in the blue cheese. Store sealed jar in refrigerator for up to 1 week. Not only should the quintessential wedge salad be served with this luscious dressing, but it is also excellent alongside chicken wings and makes a delicious topping for baked potatoes. Makes a generous 1 cup.

HONEY MUSTARD DRESSING

⅓ cup	**Dijon mustard**
¼ cup	**honey**
¼ cup	**apple cider vinegar**
1½ teaspoons	**kosher salt**
	salt and pepper, to taste
¼ cup	**olive oil**

Combine all ingredients except olive oil in a pint jar, secure lid, and shake. Remove lid, add olive oil, secure lid, and shake vigorously to emulsify. Store sealed jar in refrigerator for up to 1 week. This is super tasty on spinach salad with hard-boiled eggs, or as dip for chicken strips. It also makes a great baste for chicken, pork, and salmon. Makes 1 cup.

CLASSIC FRENCH VINAIGRETTE

2 tablespoons	**finely minced shallot**
1 teaspoon	**finely minced garlic**
1/4 cup	**red wine vinegar**
2 teaspoons	**Dijon mustard**
	salt and pepper, to taste
1/2 cup	**olive oil**

Combine all ingredients except olive oil in a pint jar, secure lid, and shake. Remove lid, add olive oil, secure lid, and shake vigorously to emulsify. Store sealed jar in refrigerator for up to 1 week. Makes scant 1 cup.

SOUTHERN-STYLE BBQ SPICE BLEND

½ cup	**paprika**
¼ cup	**kosher salt**
¼ cup	**freshly ground black pepper**
¼ cup	**brown sugar**
¼ cup	**chile powder**
3 tablespoons	**ground cumin**
2 tablespoons	**ground coriander**
1 tablespoon	**cayenne pepper,** or to taste

Spoon all ingredients into a pint jar. Secure lid and shake to blend spices. Store sealed jar at room temperature for up to 6 months. Use to season meats and chicken or as a dry rub to marinade ribs, chicken, or pork chops. As a dry rub, sprinkle 1–2 tablespoons onto food and rub in. As a marinade, combine ¼ cup olive and 1–2 tablespoons spice blend, mix well, and pour onto meat. Allow both dry rub and marinade to season meats at least 1 hour or up to 12 hours before cooking; for fish, only for 1 hour. Makes 2 cups.

RASPBERRY VINAIGRETTE

2 tablespoons	**raspberry jam**
4 tablespoons	**red wine vinegar**
	salt and pepper, to taste
½ cup	**olive oil**

Combine all ingredients except olive oil in a pint jar, secure lid, and shake. Remove lid, add olive oil, secure lid, and shake vigorously to emulsify. Store sealed jar in refrigerator for up to 1 week. Makes scant 1 cup.

MEXICAN SPICE BLEND

2 tablespoons	**sugar**
1 $\frac{1}{2}$	**teaspoons salt**
2 tablespoons	**chili powder**
3 teaspoons	**cumin**
3 teaspoons	**paprika**
1 teaspoon	**garlic powder**
1 teaspoon	**onion powder**

Spoon all ingredients into a half-pint jar. Secure lid and shake to blend spices. Store sealed jar at room temperature for up to 6 months. Use to season tacos, enchiladas, rice, and beans. Stir into sour cream for a great Mexican-inspired dip. Use as dry rub for fajitas, chicken, and fish. Makes $\frac{1}{2}$ cup.

GREEK SPICE BLEND

4 teaspoons	**onion powder**
4 teaspoons	**garlic powder**
2 tablespoons	**dried oregano**
4 teaspoons	**dried basil**
2 teaspoons	**dried dill**
2 teaspoon	**salt**
2 teaspoons	**pepper**

Spoon all ingredients into a half-pint jar. Secure lid and shake to blend spices. Store sealed jar at room temperature for up to 6 months. Use to season ground meat for stuffed bell peppers or hamburgers, stir into Greek yogurt for a dip, or sprinkle on grilled potatoes. Makes scant 1/2 cup.

MOROCCAN SPICE BLEND

4 teaspoons	**paprika**
4 teaspoons	**cumin**
2 teaspoons	**ground cinnamon**
I teaspoon	**ground ginger**
I teaspoon	**salt**
2 teaspoons	**pepper**
2 tablespoons	**brown sugar**
I teaspoon	**ground cloves**
$^{1}/_{4}$–$^{1}/_{2}$ teaspoon	**cayenne pepper**

Spoon all ingredients into a half-pint jar. Secure lid and shake to blend spices. Store sealed jar at room temperature for up to 6 months. Use to season shrimp, chicken, lamb, beef, chickpeas, and rice. Makes $^{1}/_{2}$ cup.

SEEDED HONEY

I cup	**honey**
I tablespoon	**black sesame seeds,** lightly toasted
2 tablespoons	**white sesame seeds,** lightly toasted
I tablespoon	**poppy seeds**
I tablespoon	**coriander seeds,** lightly toasted and crushed
½ teaspoon	**cardamom seeds,** lightly toasted and crushed
2 tablespoons	**sunflower seeds,** lightly toasted

Pour the honey into a pint jar. Add the seeds and stir well. Secure lid and keep at room temperature for up to 5 days, or refrigerate for up to I month. If refrigerated, allow to come to room temperature before using. Drizzle over oatmeal or freshly-baked bread, use as a topping for yogurt, or spoon on top of goat cheese for a great charcuterie board addition. Makes I generous cup.

VARIATION: Other great seed options are chia and flax; mix and match to your taste.

HOT HONEY

 2 **hot chiles,** such as Fresno,
        habanero, or Thai, thinly sliced
 I cup **honey**

Place the peppers in a pint jar. Pour the honey over the peppers and
heat in microwave for 30–45 seconds in 15-second intervals until
honey has warmed. Set aside for I hour to infuse. Remove peppers and
secure lid. Keep at room temperature for up to 5 days, or refrigerate
for up to I month. If refrigerated, allow to come to room temperature
before using. Great on wings, fried chicken, BBQ ribs, pork, salmon, or
shrimp. Makes I cup.

CLASSIC TOMATO SAUCE

¾ cup	**tomato paste**
2 tablespoons	**minced garlic**
1 tablespoon	**dried basil**
1 tablespoon	**dried oregano**
1 tablespoon	**dried parsley**
1 cup	**crushed tomatoes**
	salt and pepper, to taste

Combine all ingredients in a pint jar and shake well to combine. Store sealed jar in refrigerator for up to 1 week. Add to cooked ground meat for a quick spaghetti sauce, serve over chicken parmesan, or use it as a pizza sauce. Makes 1 cup.

PRESTO PESTO SAUCE

1 cup	**fresh basil,** minced
2 tablespoons	**minced garlic**
1/2 cup	**finely chopped pine nuts** or walnuts
1/2 cup	**grated Parmesan cheese**
1/4 cup	**freshly squeezed lemon juice**
1 cup	**olive oil**
	salt and pepper, to taste

Combine all ingredients in a quart jar and shake well to combine. Delicious on pasta, stirred into sour cream for a dip to serve with chips or veggies, or mixed into tuna salad. Store sealed jar in refrigerator for up to 1 week. Makes 2 cups.

FETTUCCINI ALFREDO SAUCE

¹/₂ cup	**melted butter**
2 tablespoons	**minced garlic**
2 cups	**grated Parmesan cheese**
I teaspoon	**white pepper**
¹/₂ cup	**full-fat sour cream**
¹/₂ cup	**heavy cream**
	salt and pepper, to taste

Combine all ingredients in a quart jar and shake well to combine.
Store sealed jar in refrigerator for up to I week. Pour into a saucepan
and heat before using. Delicious on all pastas and grilled chicken.
Makes 2¹/₂ cups.

ASIAN PEANUT SAUCE

1 cup	**peanut butter**
1 tablespoon	**minced garlic**
1 teaspoon	**light brown sugar**
1 tablespoon	**minced fresh ginger**
1 teaspoon	**freshly squeezed lime juice**
1/2 cup	**reduced-sodium soy sauce**
1/2 cup	**chopped scallion**
1 tablespoon	**Sriracha sauce**
1 cup	**water**

Combine all ingredients in a quart jar and shake well to combine. Store sealed jar in refrigerator for up to 1 week. Stir into cooked shrimp or chicken dishes with rice noodles or jasmine rice. Makes 2 1/2 cups.

HERBES DE PROVENCE SPICE BLEND

3 tablespoons	**dried thyme**
2 tablespoons	**dried savory**
2 tablespoons	**dried oregano**
1 tablespoon	**dried rosemary**
1 tablespoon	**dried marjoram**
2 tablespoons	**dried parsley**
1 tablespoon	**dried culinary lavender**
	(optional but recommended)

Spoon all ingredients into a half-pint jar. Secure lid and shake to blend spices. Store sealed jar at room temperature for up to 6 months. Use to season roast turkey and chicken and roasted veggies like carrots, onions, squash, and tomatoes.

GIFT-GIVING JARS

M&M'S COOKIE MIX

1 1/2 cups	**flour**
1 teaspoon	**baking powder**
1/2 teaspoon	**baking soda**
1/4 teaspoon	**salt**
1 cup	**M&M's**
1/3 cup	**firmly packed light brown sugar**
1/2 cup	**sugar**

In a bowl, whisk together the flour, baking powder, baking soda, and salt. Spoon into the bottom of a wide-mouth quart jar. Add M&M's, dropping in lightly so that they don't sink into the flour. Top M&M's with brown sugar and granulated sugar. As you add each layer, tap jar lightly on countertop to level the ingredients. Secure lid and decorate as desired, attaching a tag or notecard with the jar ingredients listed and directions below for baking.

Pour contents of jar into a large bowl and stir to combine. Add 1/2 cup melted and slightly cooled unsalted butter, 1 beaten egg, and 2 teaspoons vanilla. Stir until combined. Chill for 30 minutes or longer.

Preheat oven to 350 degrees. Line a baking sheet with parchment paper and set aside until ready to use.

Remove dough from refrigerator. Make golf ball–sized portions of dough and place onto prepared pan. Bake for 8–10 minutes, until the centers of the cookies are just barely set. Cool pan on a wire rack for 10 minutes before removing cookies. Makes 2 dozen cookies.

VARIATION: Use seasonal M&M's for Halloween, Christmas, Valentine's, or Easter.

GINGERBREAD COOKIE MIX

3 1/4 cups	**flour,** divided
1 teaspoon	**baking soda**
1 teaspoon	**baking powder**
1 cup	**brown sugar**
2 teaspoons	**ground ginger**
1 teaspoon	**ground cloves**
1 teaspoon	**ground allspice**
1 teaspoon	**ground cinnamon**

In a bowl, whisk together 2 cups of flour, baking soda, and baking powder. Spoon into the bottom of a wide-mouth quart jar. Spoon the brown sugar on top of the flour. Whisk together the remaining 1 1/4 cups flour with the ginger, cloves, allspice, and cinnamon; spoon on top of the brown sugar. As you add each layer, tap jar lightly on countertop to level the ingredients. Secure lid and decorate as desired, attaching a tag or notecard with the jar ingredients listed and directions below for baking.

Mix contents of the jar with 1/2 cup melted butter, 2 lightly beaten eggs, and 1 cup molasses. Cover dough and refrigerate for 2 hours or overnight.

Preheat oven to 350 degrees. Line a baking sheet with parchment paper and set aside until ready to use.

Remove dough from refrigerator. Lightly flour a surface and roll the cold dough no thicker than 1/4 inch. Cut out desired shapes. Place the cookies on the prepared pan 1 1/2–2 inches apart. Bake the cookies for 10–12 minutes depending on the size of the cookie. Cool pan on a wire rack and remove cookies after 5 minutes. Decorate when completely cooled. Makes 2 dozen cookies.

HOMEMADE CORNBREAD MIX

1 cup	**flour**
1 cup	**yellow cornmeal**
1/2 cup	**sugar**
1 teaspoon	**salt**
3 teaspoons	**baking powder**
1/8 teaspoon	**cayenne pepper** (optional)

Place all the ingredients in a quart jar. Secure lid and shake to blend.

Decorate jar as desired, attaching a tag or notecard with the jar ingredients listed and directions below for baking.

Preheat oven to 400 degrees. Grease a 9-inch loaf pan or a 10-inch cast iron skillet. Place in oven while it's preheating.

In a large bowl, combine the jar mix with 1 egg, 1 cup milk, and 1/3 cup vegetable oil. Stir to combine, but be careful not to overmix. Bake for 25–30 minutes, until top is golden brown and toothpick inserted in center comes out clean. Remove from oven and cool on a wire rack for 10 minutes before slicing. Makes 8 servings.

BARLEY SOUP MIX

1 cup	**barley,** uncooked
½ cup	**sun-dried tomatoes**
1 tablespoon	**dried onion flakes**
1 tablespoon	**dried minced garlic**
1 tablespoon	**dried basil**
1 tablespoon	**dried oregano**
1 tablespoon	**dried parsley**
1 cube	**vegetable bouillon,** with wrapper

In a pint jar, carefully layer all ingredients in the order listed. Secure lid. Decorate jar as desired, attaching a tag or notecard with the jar ingredients listed and directions below for cooking.

Remove wrapper from bouillon cube. Add the cube and jar mix to a saucepan with 4 cups water and 1 can (14 ounces) diced tomatoes. Bring to a boil over high heat, reduce heat to low, and simmer until the barley is tender, about 20 minutes. Serve topped with grated Parmesan cheese and fresh basil. Season to taste. Makes 4 servings.

OATMEAL-CHOCOLATE CHIP BREAD MIX

2 cups	**flour**
I cup	**rolled oats**
½ cup	**sugar**
½ cup	**brown sugar**
2 teaspoons	**baking powder**
I teaspoon	**baking soda**
½ teaspoon	**ground cinnamon**
½ teaspoon	**salt**
½ cup	**chopped walnuts** or pecans
½ cup	**miniature chocolate chips**

In a quart jar, layer ingredients above in the order in which they are listed. Seal and decorate as desired. Attach a tag or notecard with the jar ingredients listed and directions for making.

Preheat oven to 350 degrees. Butter and lightly dust a 9-inch loaf pan with flour. Set aside until ready to use.

In a small bowl, beat I ½ cups buttermilk, 2 eggs, and ¼ cup melted butter. Place the dry ingredients from jar into a larger bowl. Stir wet mixture into dry ingredients just until evenly moistened; batter will be lumpy. Spoon into prepared pan and bake for 45–50 minutes, until a wooden skewer inserted in the center comes out clean. Makes I loaf.

HAPPY BIRTHDAY PANCAKE MIX

1 ½ cup	**flour**
3 tablespoons	**sugar**
1 ½ teaspoons	**baking powder**
¾ teaspoon	**baking soda**
¼ teaspoon	**salt**
2 teaspoons	**powdered egg replacer**
6 tablespoons	**powdered buttermilk**
¼ cup	**confetti sprinkles**

Layer all ingredients as listed into a quart jar and secure lid.

Decorate jar as desired, attaching a tag or notecard with the jar ingredients listed and directions below for cooking.

Add 1 ½ cups water directly to the pancake mix in the jar. Seal and shake for 1–2 minutes. Pancake batter will be slightly lumpy. Cook pancakes and serve. Makes 12–14 pancakes.

CURRY AND LENTIL SOUP MIX

⅔ cup	**orange lentils**
⅔ cup	**French green lentils**
1 tablespoon	**curry powder**
1 tablespoon	**dried onion flakes**
1 tablespoon	**dried minced garlic**
2 cubes	**vegetable bouillon**
¼ teaspoon	**crushed red pepper**

In a pint jar, carefully layer all ingredients in the order listed. Secure lid. Decorate jar as desired, attaching a tag or notecard with the jar ingredients listed and directions below for cooking.

Remove wrapper from bouillon cubes. Add the cubes and jar mix to a saucepan with 4 cups water and 1 can (14 ounces) full-fat coconut milk. Bring to a boil over high heat, reduce heat to low, and simmer until the lentils are tender, about 20 minutes. Season to taste. Makes 4 servings.

OLD-FASHIONED CHICKEN NOODLE SOUP MIX

1 tablespoon	**dried onion flakes**
1 tablespoon	**dried minced garlic**
1	**bay leaf**
$\frac{1}{2}$ teaspoon	**dried rosemary**
$\frac{1}{2}$ teaspoon	**dried sage**
$\frac{1}{2}$ teaspoon	**dried thyme**
$\frac{1}{2}$ teaspoon	**celery seed**
1 cube	**chicken bouillon**
2 cups	**wide egg noodles**

In a pint jar, carefully layer all ingredients in the order listed. Secure lid. Decorate jar as desired, attaching a tag or notecard with the jar ingredients listed and directions below for cooking.

Heat 1 tablespoon oil in a saucepan over medium-high heat. Saute 1 diced carrot and 1 diced celery stalk until just tender, about 5 minutes. Remove wrapper from bouillon cube. Add the cube and jar mix to the saucepan. Add 3 cups water. Bring to a boil, reduce heat, and simmer until the noodles are cooked through, about 10 minutes. Stir in 2 cups cooked chopped chicken before serving. Season to taste.

SWEET AND SALTY GORP BLEND

1/2 cup	**chocolate-covered blueberries**
1/2 cup	**almonds**
1/2 cup	**mini pretzels**
1/2 cup	**pecans**
1/4 cup	**dried cherries**
1/2 teaspoon	**ground cinnamon**
1/4 teaspoon	**flaky sea salt**

Layer all ingredients in a quart jar, leaving about 1 inch at the top for shaking. Secure lid. Decorate as desired, attaching a tag or notecard with the ingredients list. Store in a cool, dry place for up to 2 months. Makes 4 (1/2-cup) servings.

COZY AS A BLANKET GORP BLEND

1/2 cup	**pecans** or walnuts
1/2 cup	**dried apples**
1/2 cup	**maple or vanilla granola**
1/4 cup	**pumpkin seeds**
1/4 cup	**cinnamon chips**

Layer all ingredients in a quart jar, leaving about 1 inch at the top for shaking. Secure lid. Decorate as desired, attaching a tag or notecard with the ingredients list. Store in a cool, dry place for up to 2 months. Makes 4 (1/2-cup) servings.

MONKEY BUSINESS GORP BLEND

¼ cup	**raw peanuts**
½ cup	**raw almonds** or cashews
¼ cup	**dark chocolate chips**
½ cup	**banana chips**
½ cup	**coconut flakes**
¼ teaspoon	**flaky sea salt**

Layer all ingredients in a quart jar, leaving about 1 inch at the top for shaking. Secure lid. Decorate as desired, attaching a tag or notecard with the ingredients list. Store in a cool, dry place for up to 2 months. Makes 4 (½-cup) servings.

LET'S GO TO THE MOVIES GORP BLEND

$\frac{1}{2}$ cup **prepared popcorn**
$\frac{1}{2}$ cup **raw peanuts**
$\frac{1}{2}$ cup **chocolate-covered raisins**
$\frac{1}{2}$ cup **dried cranberries**

Layer all ingredients in a quart jar, leaving about 1 inch at the top for shaking. Secure lid. Decorate as desired, attaching a tag or notecard with the ingredients list. Store in a cool, dry place for up to 2 months. Makes 4 ($\frac{1}{2}$-cup) servings.

BROWNIE MIX

1⅔ cup	**sugar**
¾ cup	**cocoa powder**
1⅓ cup	**flour**
½ teaspoon	**baking powder**
¼ teaspoon	**salt**
¾ cup	**chocolate chips**
¼ cup	**chopped walnuts** (optional, substitute with more chocolate chips if omitting)

In a bowl, whisk together the sugar and cocoa powder. Spoon into the bottom of a wide-mouth quart jar. Layer the rest of the ingredients: flour, baking powder, salt, chocolate chips, and walnuts. Secure lid and decorate as desired, attaching a tag or notecard with the jar ingredients listed and directions below for baking.

Preheat oven to 350 degrees. Line a 9 x 13-inch pan with foil, allowing 2 inches on each end as an overlap. Spray with cooking spray and set aside until ready to use.

In a medium bowl, add ¾ cup melted and slightly cooled butter, 2 eggs, 2 tablespoons coffee or water, and 2 teaspoons vanilla.

Stir well to combine. Spread into prepared pan and bake for 20–25 minutes. Cool on a wire rack for 15 minutes, and then remove the brownie with the foil handles. Cool for another 20–30 minutes, remove foil, and slice. Makes 12 brownies.

NOTES

NOTES

NOTES

NOTES

NOTES

NOTES

NOTES

NOTES

METRIC CONVERSION CHART

Volume Measurements		Weight Measurements		Temperature Conversion	
U.S.	Metric	U.S.	Metric	Fahrenheit	Celsius
1 teaspoon	5 ml	1/2 ounce	15 g	250	120
1 tablespoon	15 ml	1 ounce	30 g	300	150
1/4 cup	60 ml	3 ounces	90 g	325	160
1/3 cup	75 ml	4 ounces	115 g	350	180
1/2 cup	125 ml	8 ounces	225 g	375	190
2/3 cup	150 ml	12 ounces	350 g	400	200
3/4 cup	175 ml	1 pound	450 g	425	220
1 cup	250 ml	2 1/4 pounds	1 kg	450	230

 Check out these "101" favorites
for more tasty recipes:

Bacon	**More Bacon**
Beans	**More Ramen**
Beer	**More Slow Cooker**
Bundt® Cake	**Pumpkin**
Cake Mix	**Ramen Noodles**
Canned Biscuits	**Rice**
Casserole	**Sheet Pan**
Chile Peppers	**Slow Cooker**
Dutch Oven	**Toaster Oven**
Grits	**Tortilla**
Instant Pot®	**Tots**

Each 128 pages, $9.99

Available at bookstores or directly from GIBBS SMITH
1.800.835.4993
www.gibbs-smith.com

ABOUT THE AUTHOR

Barbara Beery founded Batter Up Kids in 1991, and has since taught thousands of children the joy of cooking through year-round classes, cooking birthday parties and summer cooking camps. She has written almost a dozen cookbooks, appeared twice on the *Today Show*, *CBN* with Pat Robertson and her business has been featured in the *New York Times* and *Entrepreneur* Magazine, as well as dozens of other local and national publications.

Barbara believes in teaching children about giving back to their community. She is currently working closely with and has the endorsement of Rachael Ray's Yum-o Organization, Susan G. Komen, American Heart Association, and the Great American Bake Sale. She lives in Austin, TX.